Ru

by Iain Gray

Lang**Syne**

PUBLISHING

WRITING *to* REMEMBER

79 Main Street, Newtongrange,
Midlothian EH22 4NA
Tel: 0131 344 0414   Fax: 0845 075 6085
E-mail: info@lang-syne.co.uk
www.langsyneshop.co.uk

Design by Dorothy Meikle
Printed by Printwell Ltd
© Lang Syne Publishers Ltd 2016

All rights reserved. No part of this publication may be reproduced, stored
or introduced into a retrieval system, or transmitted in any form or by any
means (electronic, mechanical, photocopying, recording or otherwise) without
the prior written permission of Lang Syne Publishers Ltd.

ISBN 978-1-85217-595-5

Russell

MOTTO:
What will be will be.

CREST:
A goat.

NAME variations include:
Rossell
Roussel

Chapter one:

The origins of popular surnames

by George Forbes and Iain Gray

If you don't know where you came from, you won't know where you're going is a frequently quoted observation and one that has a particular resonance today when there has been a marked upsurge in interest in genealogy, with increasing numbers of people curious to trace their family roots.

Main sources for genealogical research include census returns and official records of births, marriages and deaths – and the key to unlocking the detail they contain is obviously a family surname, one that has been 'inherited' and passed from generation to generation.

No matter our station in life, we all have a surname – but it was not until about the middle of the fourteenth century that the practice of being identified by a particular surname became commonly established throughout the British Isles.

Previous to this, it was normal for a person to be identified through the use of only a forename.

But as population gradually increased and there were many more people with the same forename, surnames were adopted to distinguish one person, or community, from another.

Many common English surnames are patronymic in origin, meaning they stem from the forename of one's father – with 'Johnson,' for example, indicating 'son of John.'

It was the Normans, in the wake of their eleventh century conquest of Anglo-Saxon England, a pivotal moment in the nation's history, who first brought surnames into usage – although it was a gradual process.

For the Normans, these were names initially based on the title of their estates, local villages and chateaux in France to distinguish and identify these landholdings.

Such grand descriptions also helped enhance the prestige of these warlords and generally glorify their lofty positions high above the humble serfs slaving away below in the pecking order who had only single names, often with Biblical connotations as in Pierre and Jacques.

The only descriptive distinctions among the peasantry concerned their occupations, like 'Pierre the swineherd' or 'Jacques the ferryman.'

Roots of surnames that came into usage in England not only included Norman-French, but also Old French, Old Norse, Old English, Middle English, German, Latin, Greek, Hebrew and the Gaelic languages of the Celts.

The Normans themselves were originally Vikings, or 'Northmen', who raided, colonised and eventually settled down around the French coastline.

The had sailed up the Seine in their longboats in 900AD under their ferocious leader Rollo and ruled the roost in north eastern France before sailing over to conquer England in 1066 under Duke William of Normandy – better known to posterity as William the Conqueror, or King William I of England.

Granted lands in the newly-conquered England, some of their descendants later acquired territories in Wales, Scotland and Ireland – taking not only their own surnames, but also the practice of adopting a surname, with them.

But it was in England where Norman rule and custom first impacted, particularly in relation to the adoption of surnames.

This is reflected in the famous *Domesday Book*, a massive survey of much of England and Wales, ordered by William I, to determine who owned what, what it was worth and therefore how much they were liable to pay in taxes to the voracious Royal Exchequer.

Completed in 1086 and now held in the National Archives in Kew, London, 'Domesday' was an Old English word meaning 'Day of Judgement.'

This was because, in the words of one contemporary chronicler, "its decisions, like those of the Last Judgement, are unalterable."

It had been a requirement of all those English landholders – from the richest to the poorest – that they identify themselves for the purposes of the survey and for future reference by means of a surname.

This is why the *Domesday Book*, although written in Latin as was the practice for several centuries with both civic and ecclesiastical records, is an invaluable source for the early appearance of a wide range of English surnames.

Several of these names were coined in connection with occupations.

These include Baker and Smith, while Cooks, Chamberlains, Constables and Porters were to be found carrying out duties in large medieval households.

The church's influence can be found in names such as Bishop, Friar and Monk while the popular name of Bennett derives from the late fifth to mid-sixth century Saint Benedict, founder of the Benedictine order of monks.

The early medical profession is represented by Barber, while businessmen produced names that include Merchant and Sellers.

Down at the village watermill, the names that cropped up included Millar/Miller, Walker and Fuller, while other self-explanatory trades included Cooper, Tailor, Mason and Wright.

Even the scenery was utilised as in Moor, Hill, Wood and Forrest – while the hunt and the chase supplied names that include Hunter, Falconer, Fowler and Fox.

Colours are also a source of popular surnames, as in Black, Brown, Gray/Grey, Green and White, and would have denoted the colour of the clothing the person habitually wore or, apart from the obvious exception of 'Green', one's hair colouring or even complexion.

The surname Red developed into Reid, while

Blue was rare and no-one wanted to be associated with yellow.

Rather self-important individuals took surnames that include Goodman and Wiseman, while physical attributes crept into surnames such as Small and Little.

Many families proudly boast the heraldic device known as a Coat of Arms, as featured on our front cover.

The central motif of the Coat of Arms would originally have been what was borne on the shield of a warrior to distinguish himself from others on the battlefield.

Not featured on the Coat of Arms, but highlighted on page three, is the family motto and related crest – with the latter frequently different from the central motif.

Adding further variety to the rich cultural heritage that is represented by surnames is the appearance in recent times in lists of the 100 most common names found in England of ones that include Khan, Patel and Singh – names that have proud roots in the vast sub-continent of India.

Echoes of a far distant past can still be found in our surnames and they can be borne with pride in commemoration of our forebears.

Chapter two:

In the wake of conquest

A name of truly ancient roots, 'Russell' derives from what was the Norman nickname for someone with red hair or noted for a particularly ruddy complexion.

Derived from the Old French 'ros', meaning 'red' and with spelling variations that include 'Rossell' and 'Roussel', the name originally indicated 'the red haired or ruddish skinned one.'

Popularised as a surname in England in the wake of the Norman Conquest of 1066 – along with many other names – this means that flowing through the veins of its bearers today may well be the blood of those warriors who played key roles in one of the most pivotal events in the nation's history.

By 1066, England had become a nation with several powerful competitors to the throne.

In what were extremely complex family, political and military machinations, the Anglo-Saxon monarch was Harold II, who had succeeded to the throne following the death of Edward the Confessor.

But his right to the throne was contested by

two powerful competitors – his brother-in-law King Harold Hardrada of Norway, in alliance with Tostig, Harold II's brother, and Duke William II of Normandy.

In what has become known as The Year of Three Battles, Hardrada invaded England and gained victory over the English king on September 20 at the battle of Fulford, in Yorkshire.

Five days later, however, Harold II decisively defeated his brother-in-law and brother at the battle of Stamford Bridge.

But he had little time to celebrate his victory, having to immediately march south from Yorkshire to encounter a mighty invasion force, led by Duke William of Normandy that had landed at Hastings, in East Sussex.

Harold's battle-hardened but exhausted force of Anglo-Saxon soldiers confronted the Normans on October 14, with Harold drawing up a strong defensive position, at the top of Senlac Hill, building a shield wall to repel Duke William's cavalry and infantry.

The Normans suffered heavy losses, but through a combination of the deadly skill of their archers and the ferocious determination of their cavalry they eventually won the day.

Anglo-Saxon morale had collapsed on the

battlefield as word spread through the ranks that Harold, the last of the Anglo-Saxon monarchs, had been killed.

William was declared King of England on December 25, and the complete subjugation of his Anglo-Saxon subjects followed.

Those Normans who had fought on his behalf were rewarded with the lands of Anglo-Saxons, many of whom sought exile abroad as mercenaries.

Within an astonishingly short space of time, Norman manners, customs and law were imposed on England – laying the basis for what subsequently became established 'English' custom and practice.

Among those who had fought on William's behalf at the battle of Hastings was Hugue de Roussel, who was rewarded with lands in Dorset – the region with which early bearers of the Russell name are particularly identified.

The name came to figure prominently in the frequently turbulent historical record, not least due to the fact that it is the family name of the Dukes of Bedford – whose magnificent seat is Woburn Abbey, the country house and estate in Woburn, Bedfordshire, that today features major attractions that include Woburn Safari Park and Golf Club.

One early and famous son of this family was John Russell, 1st Earl of Bedford, born in about 1485 at Berwick-by-Swyre, Dorset.

He came to hold some of the highest offices in the land and was at the centre of key moments in his nation's history – serving under Henry VII, Henry VIII and Edward VI.

Described by one source as 'one of the most accomplished gentlemen of his time', he was appointed a Gentleman of the Privy Chamber to Henry VII.

As reward for his services to Henry VIII during the Dissolution of the Monasteries in the 1530s – a result of the monarch's decisive break from the authority of the Roman Catholic Church and its associated religious orders – he was granted what had been the Cistercian Order's property of Woburn Abbey and its estates, the area of London now known as Covent Garden and the town of Tavistock, West Devon.

Other posts held during his long service to his monarchs include those of Lord Privy Seal and Lord High Admiral.

Created Earl of Bedford in 1550 by the young Edward VI, he died in 1555.

His son and heir, Francis Russell, 2nd Earl of

Bedford, was also closely involved as a nobleman, politician, diplomat and soldier in his nation's affairs.

Born in about 1527, he served under Mary I during her reign from 1553 to 1558 and then under her successor Elizabeth I.

One of his many diplomatic duties under Elizabeth was representing her in December of 1566 at the baptism in Stirling Castle of the future James I (James VI of Scotland).

A rather more arduous duty, however, was serving for a time in what was then the wild borderland between England and Scotland – having to deal with what were known as 'reivers', who took their name from their lawless custom of reiving, or raiding, not only their neighbours' livestock, but also that of their neighbours across the border.

The word 'bereaved', for example, indicating to have suffered loss, derives from the original 'reived', meaning to have suffered loss of property.

A constant thorn in the flesh of both the English and Scottish authorities was the cross-border raiding and pillaging carried out by well-mounted and heavily armed men, the contingent from the Scottish side of the border known as feared as 'moss troopers.'

In an attempt to bring order to what was

known as the wild 'debateable land' on both sides of the border, Alexander II of Scotland had in 1237 signed the Treaty of York, which for the first time established the Scottish border with England as a line running from the Solway to the Tweed.

On either side of the border there were three 'marches' or areas of administration, the West, East, and Middle Marches, and a warden governed these.

Complaints from either side of the border were dealt with on Truce days, when the wardens of the different marches would act as arbitrators. There was also a law known as the Hot Trod, that granted anyone who had their livestock stolen the right to pursue the thieves and recover their property.

Governor of Berwick from 1564 to 1567, Russell was Warden of the East Marches and, as such, tasked with dealing with his Scottish counterparts on Elizabeth's behalf.

Appointed a Knight of the Garter in 1564, he died in 1585 and was interred in the family chapel at Chenies Manor House, a former Russell family property at Chenies, Buckinghamshire.

His eldest daughter, Anne Dudley, Countess of Warwick, born in 1549, was the third wife of Ambrose Dudley, 3rd Earl of Warwick. A lady-in-waiting and close confidant of Elizabeth I, she died in 1604.

Her brother, Edward Russell, 3rd Earl of Bedford, was married to the highly colourful Lucy Russell (née Harrington), Countess of Bedford.

Born in 1580 and with family links to a number of aristocratic English families that included those of the Counts and Countesses of Pembroke, she was a patron of literature and the arts.

A beauty of her time and extremely accomplished and fluent in a number of languages, she is particularly noted for having been a patron of major Elizabethan and Jacobean poets who include Ben Jonson and John Donne; also a Lady of the Bedchamber to Anne of Denmark, wife of James I, she died in 1627.

It was through the death of the 3rd Earl of Bedford that his cousin, Francis Russell, inherited the title as 4th Earl of Bedford.

Born in 1593, he served in a number of political posts but is best known for having, through the great English architect Inigo Jones, developed the Russell family property granted to the 1st Earl into what is now the square and piazza of Covent Garden in addition to the church of St Paul's; he died in 1641.

Chapter three:

Politics and civil war

**The fortunes of the noble family of Russell soared
even higher in terms of honours and distinction
through William Russell, the 5th Earl of Bedford,
who was further elevated in the Peerage as 1st
Duke of Bedford.**

In common with his ancestral Earls of
Bedford, he certainly lived through interesting times,
not least the English Civil War and the subsequent
Restoration to the throne of Charles II.

The monarch Charles I had incurred the
wrath of Parliament by his insistence on the 'divine
right' of monarchs, and added to this was Parliament's
fear of Catholic 'subversion' against the state and the
king's stubborn refusal to grant demands for religious
and constitutional concessions.

Matters came to a head with the outbreak of
the Civil War in 1642, with Parliamentary forces,
known as the New Model Army and commanded by
Oliver Cromwell and Sir Thomas Fairfax, arrayed
against the Royalist army of the king.

In what became an increasingly bloody and

complex conflict, spreading to Scotland and Ireland and with rapidly shifting loyalties on both sides, the king was eventually captured and executed in January of 1649 on the orders of Parliament.

Born in 1613 – and as an indication of the conflicting loyalties of the time – Russell fought first on the Parliamentary side before switching allegiance to the Royalists and then back again for a time to the Parliamentarians before switching back to the Royalists.

Appointed Lord Lieutenant of Somerset in 1642 and also Lord Lieutenant of Devon, it was in that year that he added to his duties by serving as General of the Horse for the Parliamentary Army.

In October of 1642, he fought at the battle of Edgehill, but by the summer of the following year he became a member of the Parliamentary faction known as the 'peace party', that strived to seek an accommodation with Charles I.

The cause of the peace party foundered and Russell switched allegiance to the Royalists, fighting on their behalf in a number of major engagements that included the Siege of Gloucester in 1643, the first battle of Newbury in September of that year and the second battle of Newbury in the summer of the following year.

Because of the conflicting loyalties he had displayed, he was never fully trusted in Royalist circles.

But, nevertheless, he not only performed the important role of carrying the sceptre of Charles II at his coronation in 1661, but also that of William of Orange following the Glorious Revolution of 1688 that had deposed the Catholic Stuart monarchy in favour of the Protestant William and his wife Mary.

Elevated to the high honour of a dukedom in 1694, as 1st Duke of Bedford, and also that of Marquess of Tavistock, followed a year later by that of Baron Howland of Streatham, he died in 1700.

One of his sons was William Russell, born in 1639, and better known as Baron Russell.

The ill-fated baron, a leading member of the Country Party, forerunner of the Whig Party, was executed in 1683 for his involvement in the Rye House Plot – an abortive attempt to assassinate Charles II and his brother the future James II as they returned from Newmarket to London.

In the BBC television series *Who Do You Think You Are?* it was revealed that the actress Celia Imrie is one of his descendants – his eight-times granddaughter.

Serving for a time as First Lord of the Admiralty, John Russell, 4th Duke of Bedford, was born in 1710. He died in 1771 while, through also holding the post of Lord Lieutenant of Ireland, he was instrumental in attempting to curb the harsh penal policies then in place against the island's Roman Catholics.

A leading politician of the Whig Party, John Russell, 6th Duke of Bedford, was born in 1766. Also serving as a Lord Lieutenant of Ireland and appointed a Knight of the Garter in 1830, he died in 1839.

He was the father of John Russell, 1st Earl Russell, born in 1792. As a Whig politician, he served as Prime Minister of Great Britain on two occasions.

These were from July of 1846 to February of 1852 and, in what is known as the Second Russell Administration, from October of 1865 to June of 1866; created Earl Russell and Viscount Amberley in 1861, he died four years later.

He was the father of John Russell, who succeeded him as Viscount Amberley. Born in 1842, he was an early advocate – highly controversial for his times – of women's suffrage and birth control.

These were campaigns that also received the vociferous support of his wife Katharine Russell (née

Stanley), Viscountess Amberley; she died in 1874, two years after her husband.

One of their sons was the celebrated philosopher, mathematician, logician, historian and writer Bertrand Russell, 3rd Earl Russell, born in 1872.

A Fellow of the scientific think-tank the Royal Society and author of a number of works that include, along with A.N. Whitehead, *Principia Mathematica* and his 1966 The *Prospects of Industrial Civilization*, he died in 1970.

His daughter, Lady Katharine Jane Tait, born in 1923, is the author whose many works include her 1975 *My Father, Bertrand Russell*.

Born in 1940, Henry Robin Ian Russell, 14th Duke of Bedford, is best known for his appearance with his wife Henrietta in the BBC television series *Country House* that featured the family's ancestral home of Woburn Abbey.

He died in 2003 and was succeeded, as 15th Duke of Bedford, by his son Henry Ian Russell, born in 1962.

In contemporary politics, Michael William Russell, better known as Mike Russell, is the Scottish National Party (SNP) politician born in 1953 in Kent to a Scottish father and an English mother.

Posts he has held in the Scottish Parliament include Minister for Environment, Minister for Culture, External Affairs and the Constitution and Cabinet Secretary for Education and Lifelong Learning.

Member of Parliament (MP) for the constituency of Argyll and Bute, he is also a prolific author with works that include his 1998 *In Waiting: Travels in the Shadow of Edwin Muir*.

Chapter four:

On the world stage

An iconic Hollywood sex symbol of the mid-twentieth century, Ernestine Jane Geraldine Russell was the film star better known as Jane Russell.

Born in 1921 in Bemidgi, Minnesota, her film debut came in *The Outlaw*, after being signed to a contract by the entrepreneur, aviator and film mogul Howard Hughes.

Strict censorship problems surrounding the rather revealing figure she displayed in the film meant that, although it was completed in 1941, it was not released for wide distribution until 1946.

Other major film roles include that of Calamity Jane in the 1948 *The Paleface*, starring opposite Bob Hope, the 1953 *Gentlemen Prefer Blondes*, starring beside fellow sex symbol Marilyn Monroe, the 1952 *The Las Vegas Story* and, from 1955, *The Tall Men*.

The founder in 1955 of the World Adoption International Fund and a recipient of a star on the Hollywood Walk of Fame, she died in 2011.

Born in 1907, **Rosalind Russell** was the American actress of both stage and screen whose best known film role was that of a feisty newspaper reporter in the 1940 *His Girl Friday*.

Also the recipient of a Tony Award in 1953 for Best Performance by an Actress in a Musical for her role in the Broadway stage production *Wonderful Town*, she died in 1976.

In contemporary times, **Keri Lynn Russell**, born in 1976 in Fountain Valley, California, is the American actress who won a Golden Globe Award for her role from 1998 to 2002 in the television series *Felicity*.

Her big screen credits include the 2006 *Mission: Impossible III*, the 2007 *August Rush* and, from 2013, *Dark Skies*.

Born in 1926 in Brattleboro, Vermont, Neil Oliver Russell was the American actor better known as **Bing Russell**.

With television credits that most memorably include the role of Deputy Clem Foster in the *Bonanza* series, he died in 2003.

He was the father of the actor Kurt Vogel Russell, better known as **Kurt Russell**.

Born in 1951, his many film credits include,

starring beside Meryl Streep, the 1984 *Silkwood*, for which he was nominated for a Golden Globe Award for Best Performance by an Actor in a Supporting Role.

Other screen credits include the 1981 *Escape from New York*, the 1986 *Big Trouble in Little China* and, from 2004, *Miracle*.

Born in Chicago in 1924, Elizabeth L. Russell was the American actress better known as **Gail Russell**.

A star of films that include the 1943 *Henry Aldrich Gets Glamour*, the 1944 *The Uninvited*, starring beside Ray Milland and, with John Wayne, the 1947 *Angel and the Badman* and the 1948 *Wake of the Red Witch*, she died in 1961.

On British shores, **Robert Russell**, born in Kent in 1936, was the English actor whose major big screen credits include the 1968 *Witchfinder General*. Also with television credits that include *The Avengers*, *Blake's 7* and *Doctor Who*, he died in 2008.

An actress of stage, television and the big screen, **Catherine Russell** was born in London in 1966.

Stage credits include *The Break of Day*, *The Convicts Opera* and *Dreams of Violence*, while television credits include *Poirot*, *Waking the Dead* and *Holby City* and film credits the 1995 *Clockwork Mice*.

Back on American shores, **John Russell** was the actor best known for his role of Marshall Dan Troop in the 1958 to 1962 television series *The Lawman*; born in Los Angeles in 1921, he died in 1991.

Born in San Diego in 1963, **Betsy Russell** is the American actress best known for her roles in the gruesome *The Saw* series of horror films and in the 2010 film *Chain Letter*.

Behind the camera lens, **Ken Russell** was the colourful British film director born in London in 1927.

His many film credits – some dealing with controversial issues such as religion and sexuality – include the 1969 *Women in Love*, the 1971 *The Devils* and, from 1975, *Tommy*, based on the Who's rock opera of the name.

Also known for a number of television productions for the BBC, based on the lives of famous composers, he died in 2011.

Born in 1947 in Whiston, Liverpool, William Russell is the acclaimed British dramatist, screenwriter, composer and lyricist better known as **Willy Russell** and who started off his working life as a ladies' hairdresser.

Taking to the stage, his first play was the 1971 *Keep Your Eyes down on the Road*, followed by other noted works that include his 1980 play *Educating Rita* – which received an Academy Award nomination four years later for Best Adapted Screenplay – the 1983 *Blood Brothers* and *Shirley Valentine*, winner of the 1990 Evening Standard Film Award for Best Adapted Screenplay.

The recipient of Academy Award nominations for Best Director for his 2010 *The Fighter*, the 2012 *Silver Linings Playbook* and, from 2013, *American Hustle*, **David Russell** is an acclaimed American screenwriter, producer and film director.

Born in 1958, his other film credits include the 1994 *Spanking the Monkey*, the 1996 *Flirting with Disaster* and the 2004 *I Heart Huckabees*.

Also behind the camera lens, **Robert Russell** was the American writer who was the recipient of two Academy Award nominations in 1943 for Best Writing and for Original Screenplay for the film *The More the Merrier*; born in 1912, he died in 1992.

Bearers of the Russell name have also excelled, and continue to excel, in the highly competitive world of sport.

On the athletics track, **Arthur Russell** was the brickyard worker, born in Walsall, in the West Midlands of England, in 1886, who won the gold medal for the 3,200-metres steeplechase event at the 1908 Olympics – the only time that such an event has been staged at the Olympics; he died in 1972.

On the fields of European football, **Craig Russell**, born in 1974, is the English former player who played for teams that include Scottish club St Johnstone and English clubs that include Manchester City and Carlisle United.

Born in Glasgow in 1957, **Bobby Russell** is the Scottish former player who, after having played for his local team Shettleston Juniors, went on to make 370 appearances with Rangers.

Winner of the Scottish Cup with East Fife in 1938, **Dave Russell** was the footballer and manager who played for other teams that include Dundee and Sheffield Wednesday; born in Dundee in 1914 and manager of English clubs Tranmere Rovers and Bury, he died in 2000.

From football to the golf course, **David**

Russell, born in 1954, is the English player who, after turning professional in 1973, has been a regular competitor on the European tour.

Born in Dartfield in 1957, **David A. Russell** is the English retired professional golfer who played on both the European Tour and the Challenge Tour.

In the saddle, **Davy Russell**, born in 1979 in Youghal, Co. Cork, is the Irish jockey whose many wins include the March 2006 Cheltenham Festival.

In the much different sport of squash, **Carolyn Russell**, born in Montreal in 1974, is the Canadian retired player who won her nation's championship in 2006.

From sport to music, **Tom Russell** is the American singer and songwriter particularly identified with the 'Texas Country' music tradition; born in 1947, he has collaborated with fellow artistes who include Johnny Cash, k.d. Lang and Nancie Griffith.

Also in country music, John Bright Russell, better known as **Johnny Russell**, was the singer and songwriter best known for his composition *Act Naturally*, recorded by Buck Owens in 1963 and covered two years later by the Beatles; born in 1940, he died in 2001.

The composer of a number of hits that include *The Night the Lights Went Out in Georgia* and *Little Green Apples*, **Bobby Russell** was born in 1940 in Nashville.

Also the composer of a number of other hits that include the 1968 Bobby Goldsbora song *Honey* and the Elvis Presley ballad *Do You Know Who I Am*, he died in 1992.

Born in 1914 in Passaic, New Jersey, **Bob Russell** was the American songwriter whose many compositions include the hit single *He Ain't Heavy, He's My Brother*, recorded by British band the Hollies; an inductee of the Songwriters Hall of Fame, he died in 1970.

Born in 1942 in Lawton, Oklahoma, Claude Russell Bridges is the American musician and songwriter better known as **Leon Russell**.

An inductee of the Rock and Roll Hall of Fame, as a session musician he has recorded with other artistes who include George Harrison, Elton John, The Byrds, The Beach Boys, Frank Sinatra, Bob Dylan and the Rolling Stones.

From music to the equally creative world of art, **John Russell** was the English painter particularly renowned for his work in oils and pastels. Born in

1745 and a member of the prestigious Royal Academy and also author of the 1772 *Elements of Painting with Crayons*, he died in 1806.

To the world of the written word, **Craig Russell**, born in 1956, is the British novelist and former policeman who, in addition to his best-selling German-based *Fabel* novels, is also the author of a series of Glasgow-based novels that include *Lennox*, *The Long Glasgow Kiss* and *Dead Men and Broken Hearts*.

From contemporary fiction to early twentieth century science fiction and horror, **Eric Russell** was the British author best known for his series of work for the American magazines *Astounding Science Fiction* and *Weird Tales*, born in 1905 near Sandhurst, Berkshire, he died in 1978.

Bearers of the proud name of Russell have also lent their name to the canine world.

Born in Dartmouth in 1795, **John Russell** was the English vicar better known as Jack Russell, or 'The Sporting Vicar.'

It was while he was studying at Exeter College, Dartmouth, that he became enamoured with a small, white, terrier dog – complete with tan spots over her eyes, ears and the tip of her tail.

The cute canine belonged to a local milkman, who agreed to sell her to Russell.

Naming her 'Trump', he successfully bred her and accordingly gave her everlasting fame as the progenitor of the original professional breed of terriers known as Jack Russells.

A founding member of The Kennel Club, Russell died in 1883.